A Pet's Life

Dogs

Anita Ganeri

Heinemann
LIBRARY

www.heinemann.co.uk/library
Visit our website to find out more information about **Heinemann Library** books.

To order:
☎ Phone 44 (0) 1865 888066
▤ Send a fax to 44 (0) 1865 314091
▢ Visit the Heinemann Bookshop at www.heinemann.co.uk/library to browse our catalogue and order online.

First published in Great Britain by Heinemann Library, Halley Court, Jordan Hill, Oxford OX2 8EJ, part of Harcourt Education.
Heinemann is a registered trademark of Harcourt Education Ltd.

Editorial: Jilly Attwood and Claire Throp
Design: Richard Parker and Tinstar Design Limited (www.tinstar.co.uk)
Picture Research: Rosie Garai
Production: Séverine Ribierre

Originated by Dot Gradations
Printed and bound in China by South China Printing Company

ISBN 0 431 17764 3
07 06 05 04 03
10 9 8 7 6 5 4 3 2 1

British Library Cataloguing in Publication Data
Ganeri, Anita
    Dogs – (A Pet's Life)
    636.7
A full catalogue record for this book is available from the British Library.

Acknowledgements
The publishers would like to thank the following for permission to reproduce photographs: Ardea **pp. 4**, **7**, **14** (John Daniels); Corbis **p. 23**; Mark Farrell **p. 10**; Masterfile **p. 15**; RSPCA **p. 9** (Ken McKay), **p. 26** (Colin Seddon); Trevor Clifford **pp. 19**, **25**; Tudor Photography **pp. 5**, **12**, **13**, **16**, **17**, **20**, **24**, **27**; Warren Photographic **pp. 6**, **8**, **11**, **18**, **21** (Jane Burton), **p. 22**.

Cover photograph reproduced with permission of Alamy/Imagesource.

The publishers would like to thank Pippa Bush of the RSPCA for her assistance in the preparation of this book.

Every effort has been made to contact copyright holders of any material reproduced in this book. Any omissions will be rectified in subsequent printings if notice is given to the publishers.

Contents

Any words appearing in the text in bold, **like this**, are explained in the Glossary.

What is a dog?

Dogs make wonderful pets. There are many kinds of pet dogs. Dogs can be as big as an Irish wolfhound or as small as a tiny chihuahua.

A Doberman Pinscher can stand 70 cm tall. How tall are you?

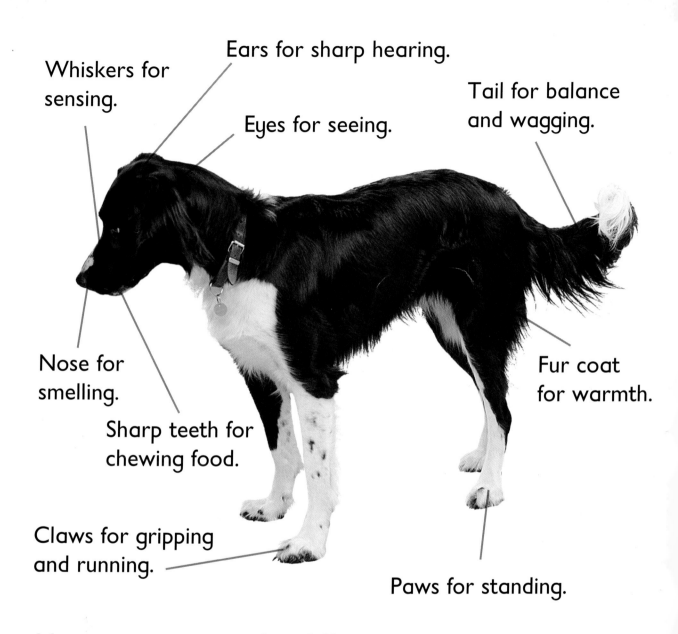

Whiskers for sensing.

Ears for sharp hearing.

Eyes for seeing.

Tail for balance and wagging.

Nose for smelling.

Fur coat for warmth.

Sharp teeth for chewing food.

Claws for gripping and running.

Paws for standing.

Here you can see the different parts of a dog's body and what each part is used for.

Dog babies

Baby dogs are called puppies. Small dogs may have up to six puppies in a **litter**. Big dogs may have as many as twelve puppies.

The mother dog feeds her puppies on milk.

Puppies must stay with their mother until they are at least eight weeks old. When you choose your puppy, make sure you see it with its mother.

At nine weeks old, the vet will give your puppy **injections** to stop it becoming ill.

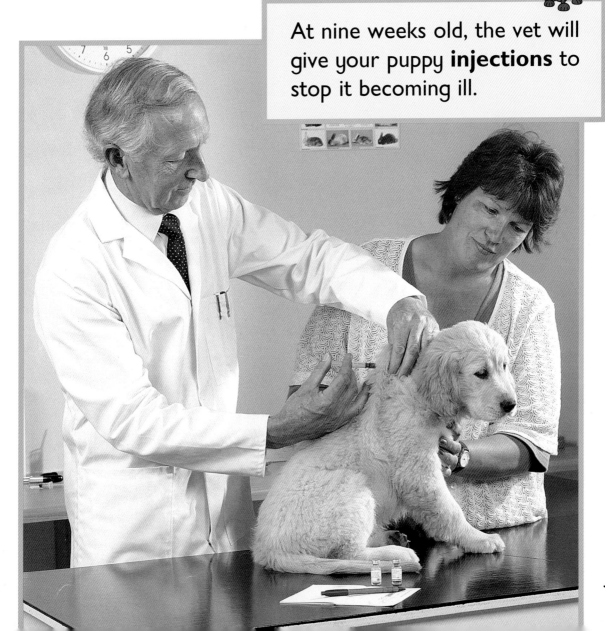

Your pet dog

Dogs and puppies are fun but they need lots of looking after. You will need to care for your pet for the whole of its life. This should be about 13–14 years.

If you look after your dog, it will quickly become your best friend.

If you go on holiday, you might be able to leave your dog with a friend or neighbour. Otherwise you can put your dog in **boarding kennels**.

Boarding kennels are like hotels for dogs.

Choosing your dog

Animal shelters have lots of dogs and puppies that need loving homes. You might want to pick an older dog instead of a puppy.

The shelter will give you advice about the right dog for you.

Choose a lively, happy dog with a clean, glossy coat and bright eyes. A cold, wet nose is a sign that a dog is healthy.

Look for an active dog that is happy to see you.

Things to get ready

Before you bring your new pet home, you should get everything ready. Your dog needs a cosy bed with a washable blanket or mattress.

A chew-proof dog bed is best for your pet.

When you take your dog out for a walk, it must wear a collar and tag. The tag should have your name and address on it in case your pet gets lost.

As your dog grows bigger, it will need a bigger collar.

Welcome home

Put your dog's bed in a quiet place, away from draughts. Show your dog where its bed is and leave it to settle in for a while.

A dog might feel lonely on its first night in its new home.

If you have other pets, introduce them gently to your dog. Don't leave them alone. They should soon become good friends.

Cats and dogs can get on well once they get to know each other.

Feeding time

Adult dogs need one or two meals a day. Puppies need three or four smaller meals. You can feed your dog on dry food or tinned dog food mixed with cereal or dog biscuits.

Feed your dog or puppy at the same time every day.

Make sure that your dog always has fresh water to drink. You can sometimes give your dog a biscuit or chew as a special treat.

Chews are also good for cleaning your dog's teeth.

Playing with your dog

Dogs like toys that they can chew. You can buy dog toys from a pet shop. Buy well-made toys that are not too small or your dog might swallow them.

Dogs love playing games of fetch and catch with balls and frisbees.

Dogs need lots of exercise. You should take your dog for a walk twice a day. Make sure you always clear up any **dog mess**.

Walking your dog will keep it healthy and stop it from getting bored.

Training your dog

All dogs and puppies need to be trained. You should teach your dog to come when you call its name and to sit when you tell it to.

You can train your dog at home or take it to a class.

20

Puppies need to learn to go to the toilet outside. Put some newspaper down for your puppy. Slowly move the newspaper closer to the door.

If your puppy needs the toilet, put it down on some newspaper at first.

Growing up

As your puppy grows up, you will get to know it very well. When it wags its tail, it means that it is pleased to see you.

Bowing like this means that your dog wants to play.

Older dogs become part of the family. Your dog will enjoy taking walks, going on holiday and playing with you.

Your dog can become your family's best friend!

A healthy dog

If you look after your dog, it should stay fit and healthy. Take your dog to the vet if you are worried about it.

If your dog goes off its food or doesn't want to play, it might be unwell. Take it to the vet to find out what is wrong.

You should take your dog to the vet once a year for a check-up. The vet will check your dog all over to make sure that it is healthy.

The vet can also clip your dog's nails so that it doesn't scratch itself.

Old age

Dogs can live for 10 to 18 years. As your dog gets older, it might not be able to see or hear as well as before.

An older dog might not want to walk too far.

It can be very upsetting when your pet dies. Try not to be too sad. Just remember all the happy times that you shared.

Caring for your dog will help you learn how to treat animals properly.

Useful tips

- If you want to pick up your puppy, put one hand under its chest and the other hand under its bottom.
- **Groom** your dog every day to keep its coat clean and shiny, and to get any old hairs out.
- Treat your dog regularly with medicines to stop it getting fleas and worms. Ask your vet what you should do.
- Never leave dogs in the car on a warm day, even with a window open. Dogs can die in hot cars.
- Don't let your puppy outside before it has its first **injections**. It might catch a **disease** from another dog.
- Dogs like company. It is not fair to get a dog if you are going to leave it on its own for a long time each day.

Fact file

- All pet dogs are related to wolves. Wolves were probably first kept as pets about 12,000 years ago.
- In Ancient China, people worshipped dogs as gods. They thought dogs scared off evil spirits.
- There are about 200 million pet dogs around the world.
- The heaviest **breeds** of pet dog are St Bernards and Old English mastiffs.
- The oldest pet dog known was an Australian cattle-dog called Bluey. He died in 1939, at the age of 29.
- Dogs have an amazing sense of smell. A dog can smell things about a million times better than you can.

Glossary

animal shelter a place where lost or unwanted animals are looked after and found new homes

boarding kennels a place where you can leave your dog when you go on holiday

breeds kinds or types of animals

diseases illnesses

dog mess dog poo. Dog mess can carry diseases so you must always clean up after your dog and wash your hands afterwards.

groom to brush your dog's coat

injections medicines that are given by a vet to stop dogs catching diseases

litter a group of puppies

neutered when your dog has an operation to stop it having puppies

More information

Books to read

First Pets: Dogs and Puppies, K. Starke (Usborne Publishing, 1999)

How to Look After Your Dog, Colin and Jacqui Hawkins (Walker Books, 1996)

My Pet: Puppy, Honor Head (Belitha Press, 2000)

The Official RSPCA Pet Guide: Care for your Puppy (HarperCollins, 1990)

Websites

www.rspca.org.uk
> The website of The Royal Society for the Prevention of Cruelty to Animals in Britain.

www.pethealthcare.co.uk
> Information about keeping and caring for pets.

www.petnet.au.com
> Information about being a good pet owner.

Index

Titles in the *A Pet's Life* series include:

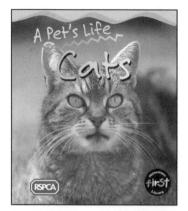

Hardback   0 431 17762 7

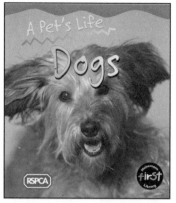

Hardback   0 431 17764 3

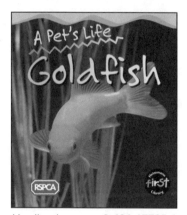

Hardback   0 431 17765 1

Hardback   0 431 17761 9

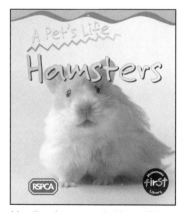

Hardback   0 431 17763 5

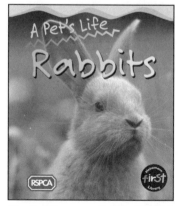

Hardback   0 431 17760 0

Find out about the other titles in this series on our website www.heinemann.co.uk/library